Leadership

The Definitive Resource For Managers Seeking To Combat Bias, Initiate Systemic Change, And Construct A Workplace That Values Diversity And Inclusion

(The Best Ways To Recognize Your Own Possessing These Leadership Qualities: Embrace Your Eminent Self)

Detlef Stefan

TABLE OF CONTENT

Wellness Communities

No matter how well we take care of ourselves, illness and injury will still occur. It is at these periods that we have to take the necessary actions to heal. We must take care of our illnesses. The best repair is a consistent one. Our bodies may recover from illness and injury with our assistance.

A significant percentage of us share meals, jobs, and housing with others. Therefore, trying to manage our wellness goals while alone is not a good idea. This is where wellness groups come in; they are essentially made up of two or more people who meet together to practice good behavior, develop good habits, or work toward reasonable goals.

Wellness clubs frequently have the same goals: You can create or organize a wellness group with a specific goal in mind. While some focus on one goal and one group at a time, others have a place with several wellness groups to cover a few different wellness objectives.

Additionally, these groups share traits and techniques. With people who share your needs and beliefs about how this well-being thing should happen, you can feel secure and free. This is especially true when it comes to nutritional theories. If you are starting to make healthier dietary choices, finding another rookie who is willing to share their experience is a fantastic idea.

Additionally, these groups will behave similarly: Consistent, fundamental behaviors are a big part of what defines a wellness group, regardless of whether members are attending exercise classes regularly or sticking to a diet together. Make it a point to determine that behavior clearly and hold each other accountable.

A wellness community's most outstanding feature is the assistance it provides. In a wellness group, members encourage one another when things are tough and give each other compliments when they're feeling lucky. Maintaining focus on accomplishments and occasional setbacks will strengthen your team and increase the likelihood that everyone will reach a final goal.

Wellness groups are available in a variety of sizes and forms. The strength of their support is what drives you to achieve more, not the quantity of people in your group.

A Question Begins A New Question

More inquiries followed after that relationship was established. After hearing the story, many were curious to learn more. Since there were none to be found, tales were created to shed light on the skymen. The gods evolved into merely stronger human beings who had many of the same vices. Some were petty and cruel, while others were kind and helpful. Everybody possessed unique abilities that governed many facets of the natural world.

Over a month, the water in the ocean comes and goes. Who's in charge of it? Well, that's what a god of the sea would do. Thus, a new deity emerged to account for a specific phenomenon. People studied in particular fields, and temples were constructed. Religion emerged.

Religion can be best understood as a type of philosophy. It's an attempt to provide cosmic explanations. All they were attempting to do was respond to the two questions that were raised. They developed the system based on the responses they received. New religious groupings emerged as a result of disagreements within the branches over the reactions to these kinds of concerns.

It is not my intention to influence you in any way with anything. Its sole purpose is to raise awareness. To be knowledgeable is to perceive and observe. Whether we are aware of it or not, philosophy is the lens through which we all see the world, and this is how we live. It is the prism through which we see the world.

I point this out to you to demonstrate how vital primitive thinking is to us. It is our identity. It's how humans function, and what sets us apart from all other animals on the earth is our capacity for reason. It is our capacity for thought. It's also what will help you advance in your new position as a manager and leader of people.

ACCURATE PHILOSOPHICAL SYSTEM OF BELIEF

You are already far ahead of practically everyone else in the room if you can grasp this idea as a foundation. The majority of us acquired our beliefs from other individuals. This is the explanation for why things are the way they are that we have been taught since the time of the troglodytes. However, the rules of the game are always there; the universe does not care, and it is up to us to figure them out. As a species, we learn more and more things that were previously puzzling. We now understand the source of thunder and lightning. We even know the exact location where it will happen. The tides in the ocean have a known cause. There is no need for and never have been sacrifices to enraged men in the sky. We continue.

For you, what does all of this mean? It's critical to understand that reality has a personality and that things are what they are. Rules govern how people, machines, and processes work. It is our responsibility to ascertain what they actually are.

What's that?

How am I aware?

How should I handle it?

Many have tried to fight against reality, but they always come up short. They construct ideas and systems based on their perceptions of what should be rather than the facts, like fortifications in the sky. Even though their reasons are false, they nevertheless want them to be. One of the most significant errors you may make is this one, yet it might not be easy to recognize. Recall that reality is the key to all of this. It is the one item that accurately represents what ought to be. Both truth and the solutions it offers are constants.

The majority of frameworks and perspectives on the world are predicated on untrue premises. Remember our cave-dwelling ancestors who observed an inexplicable occurrence and incorrectly identified a cause. An entire belief system was formed around this scenario, which needs to be more concise and probably not how it actually happened. It is tough to escape such a perspective once you are trapped in it.

You are lost if you are unable to assess the integrity of your beliefs using reality. You no longer use reality as the foundation for your understanding. It is risky to be here.

Quality of decisions

Decision-making is a skill that leaders use on a regular basis, so it needs to be nurtured. Not every leader is born equal and endowed with the capacity for sound judgment. A leader will be shaped by the decisions they make. Failure as a leader is frequently linked to a single poor choice. It is commonly linked to a series of bad decisions that build upon one another.

It's crucial to keep in mind that even competent leaders make poor choices.

Making a wrong choice makes you a good leader. How well you manage the fallout from poor judgment will depend on how mature your leadership is. It's critical to take full responsibility for your errors and avoid assigning blame to others.

How can you steer clear of bad choices?

To help you make wise judgments, you will need to learn how to sort through the deluge of information that will be presented to you. Information will be sent to you from numerous exciting sources. But remember that not every point is created equal. When digesting information, one of the first things to think about is the source.

Information is sorted according to its source. Is the source biased or trustworthy? Examine the source's motivation. For what reason are they disclosing the data? Is it to expose the flaws of another, to serve their interests, or to influence the decision's outcome?

To guarantee that the judgments you make are of the most remarkable caliber, incorporate a framework into your decision-making method and standardize the procedure with every choice. It will only ensure that you make the ideal choice sometimes. It will, however, decrease the likelihood of making a poor choice.

Five steps to making superior choices:

Analysis of the situation: present vs future. Who are the parties involved? What effect does the choice have? Which products are direct and which are indirect? Do you possess the knowledge required to decide objectively?

Consequences of the choice. Every choice taken will be made public. How would you feel if the decision was made public to everyone you meet? What do the interested parties think of your choice? Every choice has an effect on the team and the process; no decision is taken in a vacuum.

Moral sense. It would help if you always based your decisions on your integrity and moral compass. It's likely a poor option if you feel compelled to conceal it. It would help if you made decisions and project confidence by standing tall.

Benefit-cost analysis. Does the choice have more advantages than disadvantages in terms of cost and risk? What happens if the price exceeds your budget?

Scheme B. Always have a fallback strategy. What should you do if your choice puts obstacles in the way? What happens if you fall short of other people's or your important stakeholders' expectations? Any well-thought-out plan has a backup plan that works just as well.

Making long-term choices that establish an organization's mission, goals, objectives, and values is known as strategic decision-making. The actions mentioned above will also make it easier to make decisions about the organization's strategy.

Talk From The Heart

There is never a better time to be a leader than during a crisis. We had a near-fatal accident at one of the businesses I led, which had a profound impact on me and taught me a lot. An employee suffered trauma and a severe cut to his neck after falling from a motorized, one-person scaffold. My emotions and past experiences caused me to experience an overwhelming internal feeling right away, which led to actual physical manifestations. I could feel the fear-induced adrenaline shooting through my veins, my skin felt electric charged, and my mind was racing. I knew from experience that I needed to give myself a few minutes to work through this emotional wash so that my analytical self could take control of my actions and push aside the emotions that had taken control of me.

I prioritized three areas of assessment as I started the necessary interactions with my team to find out about the health of the employee who had fallen, evaluate each team member's emotional state, and consider the effects on my clients as well as the business itself.

Protecting the accident scene so that the investigation can begin is the top priority.

Priority 2: Make sure my HR staff was present and talking to the workers to reassure and soothe them with the limited knowledge we had.

Priority #3: Head to the emergency department to be with the family members who were arriving at the hospital in a state of panic and fear after just learning about the accident.

The family and I waited in the waiting room for approximately sixty minutes before the doctor emerged to give us an update. The family requested that I remain with them while the physician evaluated their loved one's condition. Luckily, the report contained the most critical information that could have been shared. The impact on the floor caused the employee to sustain significant contusions on his side and shoulder. The deep cut on his neck, which resulted in a considerable loss of blood, had narrowly avoided the jugular vein. The prognosis was that he would eventually recover completely. The family thanked me for being there for them while we hugged, cried, and prayed together. They assured me they would be alright, and I promised to keep in touch.

After leaving the hospital and making my way back to my plant, I realized several things needed to be done. My coworkers' superiors required me to know that the person was going to get better. The inquiry needed to be carried out as soon as possible but in-depth. The organization I oversaw most required to be informed, which calls for some background. The company grew over a 600-acre campus with over a million square feet of building space, housing over 1,300 employees who worked various shifts. Direct communication with the organization was difficult, but it was required.

By night's end, the investigating team had determined a few crucial elements that played a part in the accident. John was employed by a construction company that collaborated with my company. Without conducting a risk assessment or following the necessary procedures to obtain the permits required for working at heights, he had taken the initiative to install a 4-by-8-foot piece of metal onto an opening in the ceiling of an area that was being renovated (a requirement for any task being performed above 3 feet in our business).

Furthermore, it was easier to use the incorrect tool—which was already in the room—than to get the correct one for the injured person. And he had done it alone, with no one else around. Ultimately, over twenty-one factors were found to have played a role in this almost fatal incident. They would all be dealt with, but the most difficult was dealing with the culture that had initially tolerated this kind of dangerous behavior.

I was aware that it was critical to change the culture that supported this behavior, to send a strong message about safety, and to find strategies for encouraging workers and contractors to adhere to policies created for everyone's safety. It was difficult going forward to convey this message, but there was no doubt about the necessity of dealing with the matter directly.

We quickly made room in the large warehouse for up to 800 people to attend a standing meeting in order to serve the majority of the organization. In addition to setting up additional meetings to guarantee that everyone eventually received the same message within 48 hours of the accident, we swiftly modified operational schedules to ensure that the majority of those working day and night shifts could come together for the meeting.

The warehouse was filled with the sounds of movement and conversation from the large workforce that had assembled. We should have distributed an agenda or topic in advance for this first-ever mandatory meeting. I had made plans for a two-person lift, or cherry picker, to be set up so that I could be seen and heard from a higher vantage point. My ability to look as many of the employees in the eyes as I could focus on while speaking was essential to me and the message. I asked everyone to take a seat and give me their undivided attention when the meeting officially began.

I informed the staff about the almost fatal incident that had occurred. Without controlling my feelings, I told them about my drive to the hospital and the uncertainty surrounding John's prognosis. I described to them my physical response, which was similar to how I had felt years earlier when Barbara was struck by lightning and killed in one of my former businesses.

Poolside Trivia: Fostering Community Under The Sun

While resort staff set up the trivia game, people congregated around the far end of the enormous star-shaped pool. The hotel offered the winners complimentary stays in the future, so this was a viral activity. Fortunately, there were still a few empty tables to the far left of the stage, marked by bright blue umbrellas. Tom hurried to seize a table that would provide shade from the scorching desert sun and the majority of the disturbance and chatter. He gestured for Ryan to come over.

While making the rounds, a pool server in the red uniform of the resort asked Tom if he needed anything.

Tom said to the server that he would like a virgin piña colada as Ryan walked over to the table. Do you want a drink?

Indeed, Ryan said. I'll sip some iced tea.

The two men took a seat across from each other, getting ready for a more intense discussion. They were oblivious to the scent of suntan lotion all around them.

Between coffee and now, I hope you got to spend some time with your family, Tom said.

Naturally, my wife wanted to know what we were up to. Initially, she accused me of doing work, which is what we came here to avoid! I told her about our conversation for a good portion of this morning. She became excited and intrigued. She believes that I should make every effort to escape the work trap that I'm in. She also thought it would be awesome if we could improve the business without worrying about money by doing this.

Tom advised. Ryan, watch out that you don't get ahead of yourself too much. We are only scratching the surface of the necessary work. I'm disseminating ideas that hundreds of eminent business executives, consultants, and instructors have written about. The fact that so few people actually implement the views in these books is why they continue to write them. Consequently, the issues continue, and a fresh wave of readers devours the next book, only to carry on with their customs.

Recall that we previously discussed how executives feel that everyone else needs to change, not them. The prevailing mindset is, "Hey everybody, check out this book about how John Doe saved XYZ Corporation." I want everyone to read it and follow suit. Though I don't think I'm exaggerating, it's ridiculous to think this will work.

Tom, I get it. Said to be, it takes time to be done.

Indeed, but I don't want to let you down. It's encouraging that you're willing to put in the work that even just being here now. Let's briefly summarize our current situation. Thus far, we have used the three muscle groups—People, Community, and Process—to create a "muscular" framework for a healthy company. This was dubbed PCP.

Placing the right people in the right jobs is essential for any organization. A general description of human capabilities would be the amalgamation of (1) Talents, (2) Knowledge, (3) Experience, (4) Relationships, and (5) Skills. This was short-named SKERT. Using this capabilities model, we conducted a high-level analysis of you and your essential personnel.

SUCCESS vs IMPORTANCE

We are all aware that God has designated us as unique. But a lot of us need help to think of unique ways to differentiate ourselves. Let's begin by considering the kinds of lifestyles we lead. The lives can be divided into four easy groups.

A Life Preserved

A Life of Self-Deprecation

A Successful Life

A Life Meaningful

We'll examine each one of them. The antidote to the Life of Survival and the Life of Self-abasement will also be discussed.

Two Lives: One of Self-Abasement and Survival

A life of survival is the lowest form of energy. Some folks carry out their everyday tasks and move on. They act out of necessity in order to barely survive; they work out of necessity. They need more enthusiasm for anything they accomplish. They make no use of their abilities. They aren't even curious about their abilities. They are going about their lives, praying that no opportunities or crises present themselves. Richard Dawkins, a Darwinian scholar, once stated,

It makes sense that those who follow Darwin are not the ideal people to look up to when trying to figure out why we are here.

It is simple to transition from a Life of Survival to a Life of Self-abasement. Here's where self-worth is undermined. One walks about thinking, "I am nothing." I'm a vermin. I'm useless, etc. The unfortunate thing is that some individuals even use this life as justification for their humility. The truth about humility is that it involves thinking less of oneself, not less of oneself. People who live a Life of Self-abasement mistakenly believe that by being themselves, they are making a positive contribution to others. In this place, the goal of life is to give everything away under the guise of helping and improving the lives of others. One hates oneself, is unappreciative of the gifts that have been bestowed upon one, and consistently behaves in a way that belittles oneself. Anyone who leads a life like this will cause remorse in the hearts of others. This individual constantly talks about the "sacrifices" that they have made, clearly intending to instill guilt in other people.

This life is situated on the other end of the value spectrum. Even though these people help others, they have little regard for themselves and genuinely misuse the abilities and gifts that God has given them.

Individuals who live a Life of Self-abasement and Survival lose sight of the fact that God made them in His image. They fail to remember that God is error-free. God does not make garbage. Our sense of worth should come from the fact that God created us in His image. Our experiences may have brought us to this point. It's possible that we tried and failed, which is what put us in that predicament. However, the truth is that God does not want us to remain imprisoned by our transgressions, past, or sin. So that we could have abundant lives, Jesus Christ came. God loved us so much that He was prepared to give His own Son in order to reconcile us to Himself, which is why Jesus Christ came to earth.

Being truthful with God, oneself, and other people is the antidote to living a life of self-abasement and survival. Examining this three-leg stool is a good idea.

12 FORM A Tight-Knit Group

The capacity to build a team whose members are willing to support one another is the actual test of a leader's success.

In many cases, a manager overseeing a close-knit group will merely need to uphold the status quo and require minimal relational intervention. In other situations, though, the circumstances surrounding the establishment or enhancement of these ties will need to be established.

It goes without saying that one should avoid pushing dynamics on collaborators that could not be well accepted. Instead, make sure that the right circumstances are set up in an almost wholly natural way so that people can grow to appreciate and know one another better.

How often do we have tense working relationships with coworkers we don't really know or even know about? It might be that they once replied poorly to an email or that someone else merely spread negative rumors about them.

Despite our little understanding of them, we consider it sufficient to categorize them as "colleagues to avoid."

Cooperating on a project, going on a trip, hosting a business dinner, or participating in team-building exercises may foster better relationships among coworkers. Engaging in these kinds of activities enables you to live in close proximity for a while, which promotes a better understanding. But most of all, they let you work for a shared objective.

As a leader, you must be aware of the dynamics within your team. As we discussed in chapter five, it is preferable to have a close-knit group of people who occasionally disagree with your viewpoints than a group of individuals who are mavericks who are waiting for your orders and are prepared to stab one another in the back at the first chance.

Gain fans by being more relatable and lowering your guard.

The majority of people believe that maintaining a flawless image is a requirement of being a leader. Only some of the time is this the case. Your followers might not take your counsel seriously if they think you are too flawless because you won't be particularly connected to them. Individuals typically follow leaders who most closely resemble them.

Students are more likely to follow a teacher who is somewhat their age than one who is noticeably older. Younger educators are more prone to view the circumstances from the perspective of the pupils. The younger teacher is able to close the gap between herself and the older instructor by drawing on their shared philosophy.

It won't be easy to persuade those under your direction to follow your wishes if you are not relatable to them. When they are around you, they will never trust you and will constantly be cautious. They are less inclined to pay attention to recommendations and advice when they are on guard.

You have to act like you are one of them in order to connect with the people you are leading. There are numerous methods for doing this. You may pick unique events to strengthen your relationship with your fans. Engage in their activities as you become closer to them in order to gain acceptance from the group.

Another option is to make time for the individuals under your supervision during regular business hours. For example, have lunch with them or invite a few of the group's more powerful members over for supper. You can make an impression on that person and ask them to introduce you to the group.

In more dire circumstances, you can let your followers down by displaying a vulnerable side. Try defending the group against your supervisor, for example. You'll be able to win your followers' trust by doing this. This works well to gain the confidence of your followers, but it carries some danger. Successful leaders only take this action when they are optimistic that doing so will not result in their termination. You can stage the misunderstanding in order to win over your followers' trust if you have faith in your supervisor.

An Excellent Leader Or A Poor Leader?

We'll talk about what it means to be a good leader and outstanding leader in this chapter. Anyone can learn what society needs and what it takes to become an exceptional leader by doing thorough research. You will also be able to distinguish between what makes a good leader and a great leader, as well as why. You must study this chapter if you want to comprehend this and strive to become a leader from the ordinary person. It will provide you with a comprehensive understanding of how to lead effectively rather than just competently.

A great leader is someone who encourages others to achieve great things in addition to doing great things themselves. They possess the enchanted ability to impact everyone they encounter; they encourage others to achieve greatness instead of merely accomplishing it themselves. That's what sets him apart from the others.

However, an effective leader can achieve great things on their own. Should someone be able to lead well on their own, they will be considered a competent leader rather than a great one. He is capable of leading from the front by taking care of everything on his own, but he is not capable of motivating others to take on admirable tasks. For this reason, a competent leader will never be referred to as a great leader.

A strong leader inspires confidence in others. He possesses great power and can inspire others, which inspires others to believe in themselves. After that, they won't rely on the leader to get everything done; instead, they will handle things on their own. Even though followers occasionally falter in their resolve, a strong leader can restore others' lost faith. With their wounded hearts and diminished confidence, they would have been tough to do, but they motivate others to attempt such things.

However, even if his fellow men are incapable of doing great things, a good leader can. He is going to be his team's ultimate captain. He cannot be a failure; his teammates can. Even if his teammates fall short, he will succeed. Even if he isn't able to inspire his allies to believe in themselves, he will undoubtedly lead by example.

While a competent leader may assist others in their work as well, a great leader inspires others to take on their responsibilities. A strong leader will never stop acting in his capacities as a mentor, friend, and philosopher. He makes both his own and other people's duties easier with his inspirational soul. As a symbol of inspiration, he will motivate people to finish their assignments.

Conversely, an effective leader is someone who can do tasks independently and deal with any challenge head-on but who needs to motivate others. The primary distinction between an effective leader and a great leader is this.

Here's an illustration for you:

A man is attempting to catch fish, as an example. He needs to succeed in accomplishing this. He tries a lot of different tactics, but he is unable to get the biggest and most coveted fish. He goes to an experienced person to ask for assistance. He approaches a man who has a lot more experience than he does at catching bigger fish. This man is the captain of the fishermen.

The experienced man can be a decent leader in this situation, or he can be a terrific leader. Not only the man who can't catch fish with the appropriate results, but no one would have wanted to ask him if he had just been an ordinary man.

Now, if this leader is intelligent enough to impart his knowledge, he can assist the man in two ways, demonstrating his leadership qualities. He will either teach the man how to capture bigger fish or offer guidance so that the man may catch bigger fish on his own.

In this instance, an illiterate fisherman is nothing more than a leader. He'll be regarded as a competent leader if he can demonstrate his exceptional fish-catching abilities. He is obviously a regular guy, but he's also a good leader because he can catch fish on his own. If he can help the man learn how to catch fish on his own without assistance, he can also demonstrate his ability to be a great leader. Even though he is an average man, the second trait will ultimately make him a good leader. Because he can assist the man in recovering confidence in himself, he is an excellent leader.

Here's one more illustration:

Example B: There is a man who goes to interviews and doesn't get hired each time, but he doesn't give up. He approaches everyone he meets and asks for assistance. However, he also persists in making an effort on his own without giving up. In addition to wanting to ace the job interview, he also wants to gather tips from other interviewees.

You can see that the man in this scenario keeps failing while never considering giving up. Despite his shortcomings, he still possesses the ability to lead. He is approaching a leader, too, in order to seek assistance. He is unable to go to the other man's interview. He'll have to counsel the individual and encourage him. Even now, he might not be seen as a man deserving of the title of leader. He actually had the chance to take on a leadership role here. He will be a great leader indeed if he can assist the failing man by encouraging him and helping him to restore his faith. Thus, he can also inspire the man to strive more, be happier, and never give up on himself. He may also be the man who, by taking on the role of leader himself, can turn a follower into a great leader in the future.

Why Is It Important To Have A Positive Workplace Culture?

Although we've discussed the development and creation of a positive workplace culture, you might need to be made aware of its significance. It fosters an atmosphere where your workers produce better work, are happier, and eventually put in more hours and effort, giving you more excellent value for every dollar you pay in wages. People are also less likely to leave your company when there is a positive workplace culture where they feel heard, accepted, and aligned with your goal. Your workers stay with you for a more extended time, so you don't have to spend as much time trying to replace lost workers, find other people to take over for them, or try to find new hires and devote time to the hiring and training process. Your staff members' life will be more joyful and fulfilling. They're going to want to work as hard as they can and experience a sense of dedication.

The trustworthy source of motivation for a highly effective team is workplace culture. Your staff members will interact with one another more effectively and take greater delight in their work environment. Everybody has heard tales of disparate federal departments not speaking to one another. And there are severe issues as a result. That is different from what you want in your organization. The more people interact with one another, the more comfortable and heard they feel when speaking, and the more little issues are prevented from growing into major ones.

The last and most crucial reason is that your staff will be able to handle all of these other things, giving them the flexibility to accomplish their tasks as best they can. They will be able to take office politics, job-related concerns, concerns about whether they're doing things correctly, or concerns about whether what they're doing is in line with your vision. They are able to concentrate on what you paid them for because of their clear vision and a positive work atmosphere.

My team frequently brings me ideas that, based on my testing, I already know need to be revised. Recently, a team member who thought her concept would be great on paper decided to give it a try. Unfortunately, I can tell you that it is a bad idea because I tried it six months prior and it didn't work. "Unless I tested your idea, I wouldn't know it wouldn't work." We shared ideas, so I wanted to reassure her that she was headed in the right direction, but this particular concept didn't work out the way I tried it.

When there are negative group dynamics, individuals compete with one another for leadership approval or a position. People whisper to each other and have small thoughts in their little cliques; they don't give everything to the center or the general topic. Communication suffers as a result. I've been a teacher for almost ten years, and I can recall numerous instances in which my class began acting in this way. It's a complete disaster! You want everyone on your team to be able to work well together and be at ease enough to contribute ideas at all.

Additionally, it would be best if you were on the lookout for folks who are only attempting to make ends meet by using the labor of others. Everybody has seen a situation when one individual puts in a lot of effort. At the same time, another didn't, and the manager who was too aloof or the intermediate manager who didn't provide enough attention pretended that the two workers were equal. You are sowing the seeds of resentment when two people put in equal amounts of work—one doing ninety percent and the other ten percent—but they each receive fifty percent of the credit.

IQ Evaluations Aren't Always Useful

Not even the most brilliant individual can be an expert at everything, particularly if the knowledge they possess has no bearing on their culture. This implies that only people with comparable cultural and socioeconomic backgrounds can benefit from IQ testing. Aside from that, non-native candidates can never perform as well as native candidates because most tests have both written and spoken components. The most straightforward benefit of having a high IQ is that it makes getting a scholarship easier. An intelligent person finds studying enjoyable and easy, which is why having a high IQ makes one a highly desirable scholarship candidate.

Furthermore, having a high IQ is indicative of a person who can pick things up fast, is eager to learn new things, and will contribute to the advancement of their industry if they work in a job involving science or other similar fields. Nonetheless, it is widely known that a large number of intelligent individuals feel anxiety and melancholy. This may be due to their propensity to overanalyze situations and focus excessively on details, which frequently leads to unneeded stress and issues for them.

Even though having a high IQ has many benefits, there is constant discussion about whether intelligence tests are fair and relevant. It is common knowledge that people from more affluent backgrounds, with greater access to education, perform better on IQ tests; however, this does not imply that people with less opportunity are any less intelligent. The argument between IQ and EI will probably never end, but in the meanwhile, it could be best summarized as follows: "IQ gets you hired, but EI gets you promoted."

Ideas for Reflection:

1) Which would you prefer: a high EI or IQ? How come?

2) According to you, which of the two is more crucial for overall success in life? How come?

Emotional intelligence and social skills are only the beginning. Another element that you must include if you genuinely want to improve your social abilities is charm. People who exude charisma have this fantastic capacity to captivate everyone around them when they speak instantly. They exude confidence and immediately manage to delight you with everything they say. That is the power of charisma at work. There are very few people in the world who are endowed with a naturally captivating personality. For everyone else? We must put effort into making it better. Similar to confidence, charisma is a skill that requires daily practice. You must persevere through it till you reach your goal because it will require time and training. Here's how to get started if you're prepared to work on developing into the charmingly cool cat you've always wanted to be:

It All Comes Down to That Smile

A natural smile should never be contrived. A genuine smile should come across your eyes rather than a stiff one that betrays your actual discomfort. Every day, practice grinning in front of the mirror until you can see a warm, sincere, amiable, carefree, and natural smile. That smile is the mark of a charismatic person. A genuine smile brightens your features and gives off an air of pleasantry, likeability, and approachability. Seldom will you come across someone who won't smile back sincerely. When you smile, you make the individuals you're socially interacting with feel more at ease, content, and relaxed. As a result, they will be drawn to you even more since you make them feel good. Remember to keep your eyes open when you smile.

2. Instantaneous Stress-Reduction Exercises

Why, in the middle of a book about enhancing my charisma, do I need to de-stress? You may inquire. This is justified by the fact that stress manifests itself visibly in each of our faces, bodies, and eyes. Happiness is infectious, but so are tension and anxiety, and other people can detect it from a distance of a mile. Because it is so typical, we might not even be aware that we are holding onto stress. But before we ever enter a party, date, meeting, or interview, we may instantly release the tension from our bodies if we learn how to let it go.

The practice of breathing in calmly and exhaling stress out: Breathe has a great deal of power. We breathe thousands of times a day without thinking about or managing it since we depend on it to survive. However, when we choose to work it, breathing can be a valuable technique for reducing tension and unwinding the body. Imagine that you are getting a routine check-up at the doctor, and she asks you to breathe so she can check your heart rate. Almost instantaneously, this moment settles us down unless we are feeling sick or uneasy, right?

Breathe in through your nose, deeply, wherever you can conduct a series of slow, deep breaths without someone giving you the side-eye: in the taxi, in your car, in the elevator, in the building lobby. When your stomach pushes out, you know you've breathed in enough. Also, always remember to keep your shoulders still. Breathing naturally and healthily is entirely dependent on your diaphragm and not at all on your shoulders.

For a little moment, hold your breath. Imagine the fresh air you just inhaled, enveloping and attaching itself to the tension in your body. Then, visualize the tension departing your body through your nose and never to come again. Try it again and feel your body release the tension in your hands. Try it again, imagining the tension draining from your face.

Exercise your face: Our faces can become worn down, particularly after spending the entire day interacting with others. Take some time to relax in private, move your face in as many different ways as you can, and revitalize your facial muscles. You can do this in front of the bathroom mirror at work, in a restaurant if you're not at home, or even in a bathroom stall. When you execute that, it will appear ridiculous, but it does the trick! In order to "reset" their faces and provide credible facial emotions, actors frequently do this before the director starts filming a scene.

3. The Immediate Focal Change

When you walk into a room, turning your attention from yourself to the others around will help you establish an instant rapport and increase your charisma. When someone is giving them their undivided attention, people notice and react favorably to that. Additionally, they respond negatively the moment

51

they see someone appearing sidetracked, uninterested, or engrossed in themselves.

Many of us need to remember to think about this before we enter a meeting or interview. Our main priorities are a) getting there, b) locating a seat, and c) organizing our ideas. It would be best if you gathered your thoughts before you walked into that room in order to make a great impression. When you eventually finally open the door, make sure to look at each person in the room. When you look someone in the eye, try smiling sincerely. You can look for a seat once you've recognized everyone. Usually, someone will pull out a chair or point you in the direction of an empty seat, so this is a beautiful time to say "Thank you."

Another advantage of directing your attention toward other people rather than yourself is that it helps you shift your focus from any worry, insecurities, or harmful behaviors you may have.

When you project confidence instead of anxiety, it becomes simpler to portray nervousness.

E: Invigorate with a zealousness

Grinning broadly, my Montessori professor demonstrated how to spread out a mat for us. "Children, look what I'm about to show you! I will explain how to unfold a carpet for you. She added flair to a simple and tedious work with her sing-song voice, which was full of sunshine and brightness. She went into a quiet state, rolled it out with her fingers, pressed it to the ground by rubbing her palms on its flat surface, and ran her fingers along its edges to release any curls. Man, it felt like she was making love to the mat. The exchange of energy was contagious.

That's how they operate, then! I pondered. That way, twelve

preschoolers in a room will cease jumping off the walls and instead focus their energy on their task. You can direct your child's entire energy toward finishing the job you want them to perform by being enthusiastic yourself.

This implies that you should enjoy the task you have selected. Please don't put taking out the trash on your child's list of things to do early on if you detest doing it. Be mindful that any work you introduce may cause negativity to creep into your remarks, such as "I know it stinks, ugh." "Let's get this over with; it's so disgusting." Alternatively, "It may be difficult, but it's beneficial for you."

It's possible that you connected the duty to bad memories from your upbringing, but it doesn't make sense to instill that mindset in your child. As for your youngster, break the cycle. Recall that kids enjoy serving others and will do so whenever possible. I've seen my class littles literally light up when I ask them to volunteer to take out the garbage for years.

I wouldn't say I like doing the dishes. My guys had a difficult time doing them. "Isn't it so nice?" my mother-in-law remarked one time while she was washing the dishes. It feels like a gentle bath in sudsy water for your hands. Whoa. What a viewpoint. I now act like I'm getting a manicure when I clean the dishes (without the nail work). Together with my children, I tend them, and we've eliminated the negative. It's a lovely moment of bonding.

My younger child was assigned to clean the toilet when he was four years old since he was still urinating all over the floor. In order to encourage him to urinate into the toilet, I wanted him to clean up the pee. It was more of a "Hey, honey, would you take care of that toilet" than a punishment. The floor is covered in a lot of urine. Here's how to go about it. When I surprised myself by checking on him twenty minutes later, I found him singing along with the toilet paper! He was really engrossed, suds all over and in the zone. I had to grab my camera and video it because it was so adorable. It was clearly a joyful duty for him, but it disgusted me greatly.

Recall that young children enjoy serving others. They have no inherent negative feelings about their play or home chores, and they are anxious to finish their work. We shouldn't ruin it for them.

Socialism, Zeal, And Achievement

It is said that the first day of Navaratri is exceptionally fortunate. The goddess Durga's first avatar, Shailaputri, is honored this evening. She goes by the names Parvati and Hemavati and was born to Himavan, the king of mountains. She is Mother Nature in her purest form. She was Sati, the famous king Daksha's daughter, in a past life. Sati marries Lord Shiva, defying her father. Daksha takes this as a personal jab and does not extend an invitation to them for a significant yagna that he has arranged.

Nevertheless, Sati goes to the event against her husband's advice out of love for her father. She feels unwanted when she gets to her mother's house and puts the responsibility on herself when Daksha makes fun of her husband in front of all the distinguished visitors. She burns herself in the yagna's sacred fire because she cannot stand the insult. She thus takes on the name Hemavati in her second birth and weds Shiva. The goddess is seen sitting on a bull, holding a lotus and a trident in her hands, and having a crescent moon on her forehead. Those who revere her receive success and enthusiasm from her. Today's pooja will start with a rite that represents women's power because she represents achievement and earthly existence, according to Granny.

We made it to the temple. The exquisite flower adornment on the goddess Durga statue left me speechless. My grandmother's flower garland emphasized the decorating, giving it the perfect finishing touch, and I could see the pride on her face. I enjoyed listening to religious tunes while I got to know some of our family members and old friends.

We got back home around eight o'clock. After a beautiful supper that was served with love and fun, I retired to my room. On the bed was a tiny present with a handwritten message that said, "Do you have ORANGE color traits? Now is the moment to look within. Take immediate action. I opened the gift fast. The inscription on the stunning orange crystal read, "Enthusiasm, Socialism and Success."

I finally understood why my mother had given me the orange outfit that night. My mother came into the room while I was still examining the crystal and taking it in from all perspectives. "Mom, is there any relation between these words and this orange crystal?" I questioned her.

Ah, Anila. You made a good approximation. The color orange represents success. This orange gemstone stands for the qualities that make a successful life, such as courage, enthusiasm, socialism, optimism, and confidence. The characteristics of the orange color are crucial for a lady to stand out from the crowd and have a fulfilling existence.

Success is being able to bounce back from setbacks without losing motivation.

- Churchill, Winston

These ladies are typically incredibly vibrant, elegant, amiable, ambitious, daring, and independent. This rich color is associated with positive attributes like inspiration, warmth, and tenacity. Your well-being must follow your passion and succeed in it without letting other people's opinions influence you.

Proudly an Indian athlete, Deepa Malik has demonstrated that her impairment did not prevent her from realizing her life's dream. She was born in Haryana's

Sonipat. She never allowed her spinal tumor to stop her from living an active life as the wife and daughter of an army colonel. Although the cancer was removed with the aid of three surgeries and nearly 200 sutures, the lower body became paralyzed. Nevertheless, her paralysis did not diminish her bravery in winning numerous accolades in the sporting world. She has more than 55 national and 20 international medals to her name from a variety of disciplines, including shot put, discus throw, and javelin throw.

For seven years, she ran her catering company to support her family and look after her two girls. Deepa was battling her tumor at home while her husband, an army officer, was fighting in the Kargil War. The family won both wars. Her decision to seek a career in sports at the age of 36 was a turning point in her life. In an interview, Deepa cited her father's advice that "it's always better to light a lamp than to curse the dark" as comfort while she was having trouble raising her family. "You become the change you wish to see, just as Mahatma Gandhiji..." helped her to see her life's greater purpose.

At the age of 45, she became the first Indian woman to win a medal in the women's shotput F53 category during the 2016 Summer Paralympics. She races motorcycles as well. The Indian government has bestowed upon her the esteemed Rajiv Gandhi KhelRatna medal, the Arjuna award, and the Padma Shri.

Not everyone has the same ZEAL to overcome obstacles with diligence, resolve, grit, and willpower. She is the most remarkable known example of a driven and accomplished woman in Indian history.

Three games each were played in the Series. Alex Wood of the Dodgers took the mound at the top of the ninth inning with the Astros leading 5-1. When it came time for the Dodgers to bat at the bottom of the inning, they undoubtedly wanted to win the game by scoring runs. Wood recorded two strikeouts and a caught line shot in center field to end the inning. The final score was 5-1.

The TV cameras panned the crowd and both teams' dugouts as the Dodgers took the field. I observed their body language and facial emotions. The Astros supporters were giddy with excitement as they believed their side would prevail. Fans of the Dodgers wore a range of emotions, from optimism that their team would win to despair at their club's World Series loss. There was excitement all around the Astros dugout. The

Dodgers players in the dugout across the field were watching with bated breath to see what would happen. They would have another opportunity to win if they scored four runs, tying the game. Imagine if they managed five runs. In the end, the Dodgers would prevail in Game 7.

Chase Utley, the first Dodger to bat, struck out swinging. Players' and spectators' emotions become more intense. After taking a pitch, Chris Taylor grounded out to second base. Once more, it was easy to identify the players' and fans' reactions. There were a lot of Astros in the dugout that looked like racehorses holding out for the gate to open. Numerous Dodgers on the opposing side of the field had a dejected expression on their faces. The Dodgers had one more chance to win the Series as Corey Seager took the lot for Los Angeles. After Charlie Morton threw out the pitch, Seager took a swing at it. Snap! When Seager's bat made contact with the ball, he shot quickly for first base. Sadly, Seager's ground out to second base ruined the season for the Dodgers and their supporters.

Every player gathered around the pitcher's mound as the Astros dugout was cleared out onto the field. There was a joyful celebration with broad smiles. The players were yelling, hooting, jumping into the air, heaping on top of one another, and celebrating their victory. Next, the camera moved to the Dodgers' dugout. A few guys were still there, but the most had gone to the dressing room. They weren't having a party. Their expressions were ones of anguish, doubt, and defeat. Baseball's 2017 season was done.

I'm disappointed. Occasionally showing up in tiny quantities and other times ripping through our lives like a tornado from Kansas. Unfortunately, there isn't much discussion or acknowledgment of this subject in books, articles, or leadership programs. Every individual has a different perspective on the event, response to it, and method of healing. It's critical to keep in mind that disappointment is a familiar feeling. For the benefit of those, we lead as well as the leader. We need to comprehend the relationship between disappointment and expectations. Letdowns are more likely to cause a more profound impact when expectations are high.

SAWIRESS

The idea of awareness appears simple at first glance. Being aware impacts the team's general and individual emotional well-being as we well-being accomplish our tasks, making it a complex and constantly changing process for the servant leader. This suggests that rather than viewing their followers as cogs in a machine, a leader needs to invest time in getting to know them as individuals. External pressure is a significant cause of team conflict; a team member who is having financial issues will bring those issues up with the group. Although awareness makes things easier to perceive, it also necessitates that a leader accept both the good and bad parts of a situation and take the appropriate action to improve the cohesiveness and efficiency of the group. There are three types of consciousness: political awareness, interpersonal awareness, and self-awareness.

Self-Awareness Within

If the goal of awareness is to satisfy the needs of others to persuade those being led towards a common goal, then the first step towards being completely aware begins with self-awareness (internal self-awareness) and how others regard us (external self-awareness). Self-aware people are more likely to be imaginative, self-assured, and confident, according to a study. They also frequently make wiser decisions and speak more clearly. In addition to being better team players and employees, self-aware individuals also tend to be more effective leaders and establish more cohesive teams (Eurich, 2018).

How effectively we comprehend who we are as unique individuals is referred to as internal self-awareness. This necessitates profound introspection and the desire to go within in order to discover our actual needs rather than just our wants. According to Eurich, some of the most challenging questions in life are where the servant leader's path to self-awareness starts (Schoff, n.d.):

I am who I am.

- Why am I here?

- Where have I been?

- Where am I going?

- How will I get there?

- What does success look like?

- What are my morals, and where do I derive them?

"I, who?" The majority of persons perform numerous societal positions, including those of kid, parent, aunt or uncle, grandparent, follower, or leader. The whole person is formed of all these features working together. A team's desired output must be considered when a leader defines who they are in each of these jobs and, more importantly, how those roles assist or hinder that production. When seeking to answer the question "Who am I?" one must also analyze the basis of their morals or sense of good and evil. Morality typically originates from personal and social belief systems and experiences. For instance, most people believe that stealing is wrong; we learn this lesson from our parents, teachers, or other role models while growing up. Some folks may learn the lesson the hard way by stealing something. Experience matters in this scenario. Even while one doesn't have to experience anything in order to learn from it, it is still possible to do so by listening to other people's experiences.

Even in cases where people are aware of the possible repercussions of transgressing moral standards, seeing failure or punishment occur is usually a better teacher than going through it themselves. It's essential to keep in mind that morality and self-identity are frequently situational and contingent upon circumstances or the individual. Even if stealing from a farmers' market is illegal, what if someone is genuinely in need? What if the apple was a child's only source of food? Even though the majority of people agree that stealing is wrong, should someone still face consequences in these circumstances? Though many will disagree, others might reinterpret morality to permit theft in order to feed the hungry.

DEVELOPERS

According to Center for Management and Organizational Effectiveness researcher Steven Stowell, Ph., there are five typical organizational issues that recruiters may encounter at any point.

1. Lack of clear direction: There are two leading causes of lack of focus, which makes it one of the most prevalent organizational issues. There are far too many roles and people who need to know why or how they fit in. People consequently grow complacent, happy to show up, take care of business, and hope that someone in the wheelhouse is in charge of navigating the ship.

2. Difficulty integrating diverse personalities into a cohesive and unified team: Teams may need help dealing with the wide range of backgrounds, viewpoints, experiences, and opinions that individuals have. This gives you a distinct set of possible problems and opportunities to deal with.

3. Failure to acquire critical behaviors and competencies: You'll come across

many industrious individuals in organizations where you work. But even with the best of intentions, industry experience, technical skill, and subject matter knowledge that many leaders possess, building a high-performance organization is frequently unachievable. Almost everyone you come into contact with, even senior executives, will have at least one if not more, leadership flaws. While some of these individuals are conscious of their behavioral shortcomings, others are not. The fact that many individuals within the organization are frequently reluctant to express their opinions honestly exacerbates this issue. Therefore, it can be challenging to assist incredibly successful leaders in addressing their Achilles' heel, especially during the hiring process.

4. Inadequate feedback and communication: There appear to be two

extremes in this regard. People either go to great lengths to avoid confronting and holding others accountable, or they seize every chance to point out the flaws in others, disparage them, and depress them.

5. Lack of awareness: Leaders need to maintain teamwork when they are preoccupied with numerous necessary operational distractions. As a result, there needs to be more communication, and leaders become distracted, failing to appreciate others, acknowledge accomplishments, develop a talent pipeline, or devote time to evaluating procedures and finding more effective cross-functional collaboration strategies. Members of the team then lose commitment and focus, feel alienated, and disengage.

Thirteen

All notes are correct. Will

Jazz pianist Herbie Hancock accidentally played what he believed to be a very pronounced wrong chord during a performance in Stuttgart, Germany, in the 1960s. Miles Davis, the bandleader and trumpet player, answered with a series of notes that gave the impression that Hancock's chord was deliberate.

Davis had improvised right away, using the "wrong" chord as his starting point to transition into the next riff. He didn't pause at all. His attention was solely on the task at hand: finishing a polished performance in front of an esteemed and paying audience. Instead of hearing comments like "Ouch, I can still hear Herbie's foul chord ringing in my ear; what a disappointing performance," you would have been far more likely to hear afterward from the audience, "Wow, that was an amazing experience!"

Change, adapt, and prevail.

"... a spontaneous behavior (collectively or individually), and therefore dependent on team members' attitudes, experience, motivation, intuition, and individual skills" is the general definition of improvisation.1. In nearly any dynamic environment, a team with a more adept improviser for a leader will perform better.

"Improvise. Adapt. Overcome" is the motto of the U.S. Marines and the majority of Special Forces groups across the globe. In many serious situations, there might not be a single advantage other than acting right away with what you have on hand. Available or limited, the resources are the resources. More than anything else, creativity, speed, and urgency are essential, given the resources at your disposal.

Using this in a leadership setting could entail admitting what went wrong and getting the team started right away on brainstorming ways to use the resources at hand to create a future. Influential team leaders and members won't need to emotionally categorize the circumstance by saying things like "It's bad" or "It's wrong." In my work with organizations and leaders, I advise training team members and other leaders to report "what happened" factually rather than exaggerate the circumstances.

"Learning the Art of Business Improvisation," an article in The MIT Sloan Management Review, listed the following as the essential competencies: "... problem-solving, communication, and expression, proper use of language, creativity, and visualization abilities."

Which examined the dynamics of software project management teams. They discovered that developing these improvisation skills can be aided by concentrated effort in three areas.

Create a culture that embraces change and is aware of it. Teams that showed a positive attitude toward dealing with and accepting ambiguity and project changes demonstrated higher levels of improvisation. Units should be assisted in anticipating and identifying changing conditions so they can make decisions more quickly and accurately.

Establish the ideal atmosphere and structure for your team. The meetings enhanced the frequency and quality of face-to-face interactions centeredaround the project. Sections were then able to react to changes faster as a result.

Provide tools and management techniques that support improvisation. Teams that exhibited higher levels of improvisation were more likely to employ agile management strategies, methods, and resources. In actuality, compared to groups that used a more conventional design, teams that adopted an agile approach were nine times more likely to exhibit high levels of improvisation.2.

An organization's ability to adapt to quickly changing dynamics could be significantly impacted by its improvisational skills. Furthermore, just as in the domains of special military operations and jazz (where they are a fundamental musical prerequisite), these abilities can be taught and acquired in organizations.

When it comes to an organization, the person in charge of particular "subsystems" will frequently become aware of the necessary changes before the leadership level does. A "first response" will be a system that enables those important people to make quick, essential changes. Of course, this system will need planning, a cultural shift, experimentation, and readiness in advance of situations requiring improvisation.

Personal advantages

A skill's worth lies not only in what it can do for you but also—and maybe even more importantly—in the person it will make you become both during and after you acquire it. Consider the kind of person you want to be when you are learning. Next, determine which particular abilities could assist you in developing your character and becoming that person. For example:

Gaining experience in giving speeches in front of an audience could increase your confidence.

Getting ready for a marathon can help you become more disciplined and mentally challenging.

Regular meditation practice can improve your sense of well-being and well-being. Consider your skills in terms of how they will help you develop your character and achieve your professional goals. Next, decide which abilities will be most helpful in that context.

The extent of that ability or expertise

A skill is not something that exists in a vacuum unrelated to anything else. Learning a new skill will inevitably lead to new experiences. For example:

It increases your self-assurance, making you feel more energized and prepared to pick up new skills (after all, if you can master one area, what else are you capable of learning?)

It opens up a world of possibilities for you by granting you new abilities (for example, once you master essential calculus, you can go on to more advanced math).

It speeds up the acquisition of related skills (learning a second language gets easier once you can speak a foreign language fluently).

In this context, "reach" refers to the general influence the skill will have on your life after you acquire it (or while you're learning it). As a matter of fact, specific skills have a more significant impact than others (i.e., a more comprehensive reach). Naturally, what those particular skills are for you at this moment will depend on your goals and current skill set.

Here's what I mean more precisely by "reach":

Develop momentum. Any ability that can increase your drive is beneficial. This is due to the fact that learning will come more easily and quickly to those who are more driven to learn. Additionally, your desire to learn more will grow as you gain more knowledge. Say you're learning Spanish, for example, and you were able to speak a few words to a native speaker. You get a positive feeling from this and become motivated to learn more Spanish (and possibly other skills).

Obtain more self-assurance. Any ability that pushes you past your comfort zone has the power to demolish your existing "model of reality." In other words, it has the power to drastically broaden your range of possibilities by redefining what you believe is feasible. Let's take an example where you are a shy person, but you muster the bravery to join a public speaking group, such as Toastmasters, and give your icebreaker speech. Even if you've always believed that public speaking is beyond your capabilities, the act of public speaking begins to transform your identity. Now that you know what else is possible, you're probably wondering how much more.

Extend your choices. A skill can be wide-reaching if it increases your options in life. For example, "just" learning to speak English well expands your opportunities significantly. Being proficient in English will help you gain access to a huge job market and a wealth of information, as English is the language with the most resources available. For me, the best investment I've ever made has been to learn how to write and speak English.

And if I couldn't write in English, you wouldn't be reading this book.

I think you now have a clear idea of what a skill's reach entails.

How about thee? Which skill would you choose to master first if you could only master one?

3. Promptness

Even though a skill can be beneficial, sometimes the timing could be better for you. Timeliness is another essential factor to take into account when choosing which skills to learn. These include the following:

What have you already prepared? We are only capable of learning so much at once. Think about whether it's feasible to add one more skill to the ones you're already learning.

What is your current level of energy and time? It takes time and effort to learn. It cannot be avoided. Do you have the time and energy necessary to dedicate to learning that new skill? One tip is to save just a tiny amount of time each day if you are short on both resources (time and energy). For instance, it might be between ten and fifteen minutes.

How valuable is this skill at the moment? Be sure to evaluate the skill's current relevance to you before learning any new ones. How come? Because a lot of what we know is forgotten. As such, whenever possible, put what you've learned to use right away. It will stick better in the long run the more you do this.

Styles of Leadership

We've concluded. Let's attempt to integrate everything. You will succeed as a leader if you follow the guidance in this book. Is there a single, ideal way to lead? Nope.

A perfect, methodical leadership style is absent. Both directive and supportive leaders exist. The order provides workers with clear instructions on what needs to be done. A helpful leader is approachable and demonstrates empathy. It sometimes works well to blend the two. Depending on the employee's personality, one of the styles may work better. As a leader, it is your responsibility to provide what your team member lacks. A coach and a leader are the same. Instead of tossing the ball, a football coach calls the play so that his quarterback can carry out the strategy. Be a mentor.

Be the mentor that your staff members need and want. Sometimes there is only one solution. It is best to be supportive of a new hire who lacks experience. It could be beneficial to be more direct if you have an experienced employee. Take your time; pick up knowledge as you go. Every endeavor you undertake yields knowledge, be it in the grocery store or the corporate world. Enjoy yourself and make the most of it. Do as much good as you can for others. According to John Gardner, life takes on purpose when one is serving others.

CAN I TRY YOUR SHOES IN CHAPTER 8?

Empathy is the enema of self-image.

FROM THE STORY OF MOUSETRAP:

The mouse was stressed and confused, but the Hen, the Goat, or the Cow showed no sympathy. They were busy thinking to themselves.

A REAL-LIFE STORY:

Every average person yearns for empathy. Whatever the case, compassion is not hard to find. Sympathetic ability is an essential component of non-legitimate authority. Colin Powell, the former four-star general and observed American legislator, is reported to have stated, "I try to be compassionate, trying to see the other individual's perspective," during a meeting. I tried to get officers in the military. When I was trying to work through a problem with a pastor I didn't know well in my political career, I would try to see what he needed, not just what I needed. I figured out what we would both require.

'SHOES' METAPHOR

Being compassionate toward someone does not entail attending to all of their worries. Being empathetic does not imply solving other people's problems.

It indicates that we are aware of, considerate of, and mindful of their issues, worries, and concerns. Indeed, we are only sometimes able to resolve other people's problems. However, we can assist them in improving and advancing.

We consistently demonstrate that we are making an effort to see things from their viewpoint. Developing empathy helps us see things from other people's perspectives, which is essential to becoming a trailblazer that people will respect and follow.

Every pioneer has a strong sense of who they are. But your inner self shouldn't get in the way of your ability to connect. Self-image is the enemy of compassion.

FOUR METHODS TO EVEN IMPROVE YOUR EMPATHY

Please pay attention: It isn't easy to listen to someone. I need to improve at listening by nature. However, I must genuinely try to listen to other people. Even so, there are moments when I want to interrupt the other person to express my viewpoint. Then, one day, I came up with a fix. I discreetly press the tips of my left index finger and left thumb against each other to make myself listen more during conversations. I should pay attention because of this cue. I look at my left pointer and press it until it hurts a little when I have the urge to talk instead of listening. In the long run, this has helped me become more tuned in. People start to open up and have positive opinions of you and themselves when you pay attention to them. Observe. It performs!

Judge not: Try not to judge someone else while you are listening to their worries, problems, or struggles. Perhaps you have no idea what they are going through or why they are experiencing certain emotions that don't align with your worldview. Be open to the possibility that they could be correct until proven incorrect.

Gossip not: Individuals put you in a position of trust when they tell you their stories. Never reveal their secrets to third parties or turn them against them. In addition to losing credibility, doing so will make you appear uncaring and unfit to be in a leadership role.

Uplift, not alienate:

1. Try to uplift the person receiving the advice or criticism rather than alienate them.

2. Remember to keep your attention on the issue rather than the person. When someone feels endangered, they become defensive and hurt.

3. Consider the opportunities for correction rather than the consequences and retaliation when there is unfavorablebehavior or result.

One of Harper Lee's books, To Kill a Mockingbird, has an enigmatic line that captures sympathy. States Atticus. Above everything else, Scout, you'll get better with a variety of people if you can become comfortable with a simple trick. You can only really understand someone once you consider things from his point of view [...] and until you put yourself in his shoes and walk around in it.

Respect and constructive, proportionate actions are energized by empathy. If you demonstrate that you are thinking about it, they will frequently think more about you and your goals. As Mary Angelou put it, As a result, if you believe that other people must remember, respect, and follow you, be sure to stifle your negative self-perception and demonstrate empathy.

Generally speaking, a pseudo-culturalized senior without an

institutional background cannot supervise a true-cultural junior in a standardized environment.

In corporate settings, it is frequently observed that junior intellectuals who possess superior concepts of business executions based on their experience are being supervised by seniors who have a lesser understanding of business execution and protocols. Because the senior is professionally closer to higher management (in the context of corporate's functional accountability), this type of "senior-junior" management relationship creates conflicting situations. The genuine junior feels betrayed and moves on, looking for other job options, and eventually quits the organization due to the senior's mishandling and incorrect/incomplete supervision. These "pseudo-seniors" must have come from an uncultured and wrong group of like-minded individuals (taking wrong lessons from bad people and maintaining the false "audacity" to assume that they are the best).

Businesses suffer latent loss as a result of these seniors because brilliant junior employees may be coerced into leaving the company through harassment. Actually, rather than treating employees as mere flatterers (with hidden incapabilities), the corporation should evaluate their "employee value" in relation to their ability to contribute to the company's growth.

From a psychological angle: In order to ensure effective supervisory communication and the proper channeling of the organizational set-up, senior employees should possess higher levels of intelligence, emotional intelligence, professional conception, and cognitive ability than junior employees. Otherwise, over time, animosity would subtly seep through the icy relationship between the senior and junior employees; as a result, there would be a higher likelihood of conflict and internal strife, which would ultimately lead to the corporate goals being abandoned. This kind of minuscule mismanagement should never be tolerated since it puts corporate profits in a "decline mode." In order to have a positive corporate culture, organizational psychology should be valued, and, as a result, policies regarding department creation, team formation, senior-junior team-up, and communication guidelines distribution should be implemented.

Business lesson: To regulate and spread a positive corporate culture, psychometric tests and techno-management assessments should be administered within predetermined timeframes, avoiding the "senior-junior" dynamic and related leadership style. Maintaining a positive corporate culture and retaining the best workforce is greatly dependent on this point.

Controlling results

Results and Opinions

Your combined beliefs in potential, ability, and worthiness (self-worth) determine your results. If we want to achieve the results we want, we need to act on these beliefs. Forming beliefs is a call to action. Since we work on our beliefs inherently, we can assume that beliefs that are unrelated to efforts are just pleasant ideas and meaningless ideals.

Capacity

Limiting beliefs leads to an underestimation of ability all too frequently. People frequently discuss what they are unable to accomplish; this is a risky habit that will severely restrict your ability to learn. Your brain will believe you if you honestly say that you are incapable of doing something since it dislikes being proven incorrect. It's okay if you're having trouble learning a new skill; keep trying. There's only one thing for sure: you still need to reach the pinnacles of your potential. Be confident in your skills at all times. Negative thinking and simple self-talk can trap you in a web of self-imposed constraints that are difficult to escape. We want to follow through on our commitments, so when we say out loud that we are unable to accomplish something, our minds automatically block that possibility.

Remind yourself to be aware of and overcome any boundaries you have placed on yourself.

Potential

Suppose they do not currently have all the necessary skill sets to accomplish their goal or do not see a straight line with arrows leading them there. In that case, many people will automatically conclude that something is not possible. On the other hand, some people think that everything is possible just because it is possible (metaphorically). Never conflate ability with possibility. Despite being conscious of your limitations, you should never undervalue yourself. In the business world, letting someone down is just as bad as lying, so you don't want to do that. Performing some essential due diligence is the best way to prevent making mistakes of this nature. Never assume that something is impossible because you lack the necessary skills or knowledge. Instead, find solace in the fact that you will never honestly know your limitations until you cross them.

It's not quite enough to think that we can accomplish a task and that it is feasible. We also need to believe that we are capable of completing this task and that a successful result is ours. Recognize that emotions of unease and uncertainty are indicators of incongruence that need to be addressed through self-improvement.

In this instance, cost-effectiveness extends beyond just financial costs (see Decision Making).

Control Results and Difficulties

Along the way, you will encounter a lot of challenges; most of them will be apparent from a distance, but occasionally you will be caught off guard. When challenges emerge, it's critical that we accurately classify them before deciding how to handle them best. There will be barriers arising from prevailing beliefs and genuine real-world problems. There are two types of natural obstacles: those that are manageable and can be overcome with enough time and effort. Alternatively, they are immovable objects that, in the circumstances or timeframe at hand, make reaching your goal incredibly unlikely or impossible. An obstacle must fit into one of the following categories in order to be appropriately classified as either a natural barrier or a limiting belief:

Although I don't currently have the resources, I could get them with some work.

Although I have resources at my disposal, I don't know what to do next.

I need to gain the necessary abilities to finish this task.

The barrier makes the result unworthy, immoral, or not worth the effort.

We can then determine the best course of action after defining the obstacle. Our ability to make more choices during the categorization stage will increase our influence because we will have more options available to us.

Collaborating With Others

Though not always, the spiritual gifts of administration and, interestingly, pastor/shepherd are closely associated with the spiritual gift of leadership. This gift is linked to providing for others. This is what sets it apart from the estate of administration and ties it to the role of pastor or shepherd. This is not to say that people with administrative gifts are uncaring; on the contrary, people with spiritual leadership gifts pay closer attention to people and relationships.

Together with many other Ministry Gifts, including apostles, prophets, pastors, and teachers, this motivational gift works. (Ephesians 4:11 and First Corinthians 12:28). This gift's bearers will take the lead by collaborating with and through others. They will frequently complete the task by assigning tasks and authority to others and organizing them. A leader will set the objectives, offer support and direction, and free others to collaborate with them to achieve the goal.

The Apostles were all tradesmen with a message to share with the world: Jesus saves. They were sincere in their message and eager to serve and share with anyone who would listen. While we do not undervalue education, it is not a prerequisite for effective Christian leadership. They set a good example for others to follow by their behavior, conduct, knowledge, and love for Jesus. A key component of leadership is having a strong sense of conviction in one's beliefs. Serving others would be the most crucial trait for a leader, according to the Bible. Matthew 20:25–28; Luke 22:24–27. A truly gifted Christian leader understands that he is merely a servant of Christ and the people he leads. (1 Corinthians 1:1; Romans 1:1).

The role of the gifted leader is to shepherd God's people, to watch over and mentor those under their care as they grow in their faith. (Revelation 4:13). The words of the church leader are not "persuasive and wise" (1 Corinthians 2:4-6). God bestows the spiritual gift of leadership on men and women who will assist the church in expanding and prospering beyond the current generation. God bestows leadership not to elevate people but to exalt Himself in the lives of believers who use their gifts to carry out His purposes.

Within the church, leadership is not limited to those in positions of authority or power. Young people can hold leadership roles. 1 Timothy 4:12, 1

Timothy 1:3. It would appear that behavior, or how one lives in front of God and other people, is another prerequisite for leadership.

Solutions for Business Leaders in Chapter Four

The responsibility of being a business leader is excellent and should not be underestimated, as has been stated. It calls for self-control, fortitude, strength, reason, clarity, and a keen sense of direction.

This is mainly because being a leader involves more than just you; you are responsible for leading others who are very different from you. You also have to ensure that everyone is driven to achieve the best outcomes for the company and is looking in the same direction.

Put another way, your responsibilities go beyond your staff, goods, and services; they also include your customers, all those engaged in your company's development, and anybody else who may come into direct or indirect contact with your enterprise.

For this reason, a leader must first be qualified to oversee the day-to-day operations of the company and be given the primary duty of directing the team of workers to a safe destination.

A leader needs to be capable of:

Establish trust: Since the leader is the point of contact for everyone inside and outside the company, they must be able to demonstrate their worthiness and ability to win over the trust of their team members, investors, clients, and anybody else who depends on them for decision-making.

Assume leadership and provide precise instructions:

- Being able to take charge and lead without wavering.

- Doubting.

- Being cowardly is incredibly important for a leader.

A business leader needs to be able to make the most challenging decisions regardless of personal feelings and allegiances.

Must take accountability for their group's performance:

Mistakes are made, things go wrong, and disasters inevitably occur. In such circumstances, what would a true leader do? Accept accountability. Being in a leadership position is only for you if you think you can take criticism for the actions of others or take the fallout from team decisions. Own up, assume responsibility, and don't offer justifications.

Because strategy is the foundation of any business's success, be prepared to be both strategic and modern. It consists of concise action plans that outline how to progressively advance the company to the next level and closer to realizing its goal. A leader needs to be able to spot trends and be aware of the more contemporary actions that indubitably produce the intended outcomes.

Provide inspiration and motivation to the team: a group that needs more passion or spirit to believe in their work will never be productive. Since the team's leader serves as the primary role model for the workers, everyone on the team is affected by the vibes they project.

Help team members' higher education experiences: In actuality, knowledge and the amount that people can learn in any environment are limitless. A leader ought to take note of these chances for learning and assist their team members in improving themselves since an employee's increased worth is directly related to the contribution they make at work. Develop talent, promote skillful learning, and—above all—leave your staff members in a better state than when you found them.

SUCCESS METHODS FOR A NEW BUSINESS LEADER

Nobody is destined to be a leader. There needs to be a set of rules or regulations that automatically prepare someone for the position of business leader.

Depending on how quickly you pick things up, it may take you some time to become acclimated to your new role and feel comfortable in it when you first take on the part of the leader in an organization.

Thankfully, there are many different things you can do and habits you can develop to help you get off to a smooth and strong start. These are the steps that are intended to help you quickly grasp how the organization functions.

Evaluate the company: When you take on a leadership role, one crucial thing you should do first is assess how and why you were appointed to the position. Is it a sign that the company is having problems? Is it because something has to change? Do they have to reach a larger audience? Do they need to catch up? It is highly recommended that you ascertain the reason for your involvement and determine how you can contribute to resolving the issue.

As the new boss, you should have a different perspective on the situation than the one that existed prior to your hiring. Your new role requires you to effectively assess the difficulties and implement constructive changes to enhance the current outcomes. Make good use of your newfound authority.

Only alter the organization's structure if it needs to be changed. But most of the time, some aren't a good fit for the position they hold. In these situations, feel free to change things up, update the system, and help your team realize how important it is to survive.

Greetings

A leader is inundated with invitations all day long. He must, therefore, decide which to accept and which to reject. This is a phase in the social skill development process. An invitation is sent to you by someone for a variety of reasons. All she wants is to enjoy your company. She may believe that having you there will make the occasion more worthwhile. She may take advantage of the chance to further her business or professional goals. She might wish to widen her social network.

Everyone who extends an invitation to you hopes that you will accept, regardless of the reason. It is, however, physically impossible to accept every invitation that comes your way because of time constraints. As a result, you must choose carefully which offers to buy and which to reject. An invitation sender receives a message with each such acceptance or declination.

A leader must have his agenda when accepting or rejecting invitations, just as there may be a hidden agenda in people's invitations to them. As a leader, you might think about asking yourself things like, "How important is the inviter to my cause? Is this someone I can bring into my fold? Can I reschedule the invitation? Is this a group that I would never, ever want to be associated with?

The particular social skill that goes into accepting or rejecting an invitation is the language you use. You should respond to each invitation with a personal note. You could express your happiness, express your anticipation for the occasion, or mention that you remember the person and value his invitation to rekindle your relationship.

Rejecting an invitation is a social maneuver that needs to be done with grace. It would be wise of you to pick up the phone and politely decline an invitation, thanking the sender, if you suspect influential people will be there but you don't think it's the right moment to accept. Usually, the purpose is to send a brief note saying no to the invitation.

Posing Appropriate Questions

If the person presiding over the meeting is adept at crafting the ideal questions, many meetings could end much sooner. It is a crucial communication ability for a leader to possess. Sadly, managers frequently squander a great deal of time—their own and others'—by posing questions that are either completely unrelated to the agenda, tangential to it, or better left for another meeting.

You, as the project leader, may be to blame for these pointless meetings because you still need to complete your assigned reading. Even though you may have a rough notion about the project, it is still just an idea. You need to learn all the latest information about the project. Therefore, you take advantage of the opportunity to learn about the project rather than moving the meeting forward regarding its implementation.

The timeline for the entire project, the agency or agencies in charge of implementing it, the associated costs, and the anticipated profit are all important questions to ask. The remaining questions to ask are who, what, how, when, and where.

Anxiety's Presence in Relationships

Consider what might happen if you overreact to stressful situations by, for example, over-preparing for a social gathering or possibly a storm. It might appear innocuous. After all, it's preferable to be underprepared rather than underprepared.

Sure.

It does, however, suggest that anxiety is present. You may have anxiety disorder if you worry excessively about something that seems very simple to people around you. What impact does that have on your relationships, particularly with your spouse? For your partner or anyone else in your life, it can be exhausting, even though it appears to be a deeper problem for you. Not everyone wants to hear about events that are overestimated or that take into account every possibility that could go wrong. While it is important to accept those around you, including the fact that they get you, this is just one example of the anxiety symptoms that can harm a relationship.

Imagine now that you overreact to situations at work as well as potentially stressful events like a big event or an impending storm. You may be carrying a lot of your work-related stress and anxiety home if you are prone to worrying about work-related issues, such as your obligations or deadlines, more than usual. It might harm your kin. It may also make it difficult for you to unwind, which may, in turn, agitate those around you. I'm not sure about you, but I find tense relationships to be uncomfortable and unpleasant.

If you are easily startled, it can have an impact on both your life and the lives of people around you. This includes feeling tense, having trouble breathing, having difficulty falling asleep, overanalyzing situations, getting headaches or muscle aches, sweating, shaking, and feeling queasy. All of these anxiety symptoms affect your physical and mental well-being and negatively impact your quality of life, which in turn negatively impacts those around you.

Therefore, you are mistaken if you have ever believed that anxiety is something you can ignore or shake off from those around you. It has a more significant impact on you than you may realize and probably more than you would like to acknowledge. Panic, fear, tenseness, and uneasiness are the results of anxiety. Because it affects you, it has an impact on every aspect of your life.

Relationships are strained and put in danger by it. It might cause you to lose connections and opportunities, as well as erode other people's trust in you. You might not even realize it until it starts to negatively impact your social interactions, personal life, and career. It can make you lose touch with the present, inhibit your expressiveness, induce anxiety, and lead to excessive procrastination. Even when you don't mean to or want to be selfish, stress can make you become that way. It can, in essence, ruin your life and rob you of joy, which is why there are numerous reasons to get professional assistance for your problems. You can successfully reduce anxiety by getting help and leading a healthier, more active lifestyle. This will help you to regain the trust of those who matter most to you. You will need to swallow any pride you may have and treat anxiety once you realize how badly it affects you. It will not only make your life better, but it will also prevent you from ruining your relationships. Aside from maintaining your health and making your life better, remembering that you care about the people in your life should be more than enough motivation to take action and manage your anxiety.